Lead, Kindly Light

My Journey to Rome

Thomas Howard

FRANCISCAN UNIVERSITY PRESS
Franciscan University of Steubenville
Steubenville, Ohio

1994 Publication by:
Franciscan University Press
Franciscan University of Steubenville
Steubenville, Ohio 43952

Cover Photo: © by Ann Recznik
Cover Design: Dawn C. Harris

ISBN–940535–73–4

Contents

Foreword

In this marvelously engaging remembrance, Thomas Howard admits to being nervous about comparing his experience to that of John Henry Cardinal Newman, lest that seem presumptuous. Not to fear. I expect that everyone making the journey to Rome—or at least everyone given to serious intellectual inquiry—finds himself checking the theological and spiritual map so carefully drawn by Newman. Even those who do not consult the map along the way may discover upon reaching their destination that Newman understood their journey better than they themselves. Certainly that is true in my case, and I gather it is true for Dr. Howard. Although there is such a trusty map, each of us must, with great difficulty and frequent doubt, make the journey on his own. Only in retrospect do we recognize fully that we were never, not even for one step along the way, on our own.

Howard is keenly aware that there are many reasons why one might become a Catholic, some of them very attractive reasons. But he knows that the only consideration that "will stand up when the foundations are shaken [is] whether something is true or not." Is the Catholic Church what it claims to be? If the answer is yes, then that answer changes the question. The question is no longer "Why should I become a Catholic?" but "Why am I not a Catholic?" When, after many years of wrestling with it, I could no longer answer that new question in a manner convincing to myself or others, I became a Catholic. Becoming a Catholic is not a matter of preference but of duty freely embraced. And, with Dr. Howard, I must add, joyfully embraced.

According to the Second Vatican Council, the Church of Jesus Christ "subsists" in a unique way in the Catholic Church. It is the most fully and rightly ordered expression of Christ's Church through time. The Catholic Church readily recognizes that the saving grace of God is to be found also outside its boundaries. Indeed it teaches that all who are baptized in the name of the Father, Son, and Holy Spirit are "truly but imperfectly in communion with the Catholic Church." For the non-Catholic Christian, becoming a Catholic is the completion of what he already is. All the grace and truth of God to be found anywhere, says the Council, gravitates toward unity with the Catholic Church. Dr. Howard as a Fundamentalist Protestant and then an Anglican, and I as a Lutheran, knew much of the grace and truth of God. In becoming Catholic, nothing of this is rejected; all is fulfilled.

With Dr. Howard I can attest that one of the great liberations experienced in becoming a Catholic is no longer having to answer the question "Why am I not a Catholic?" Many non-Catholic Christians, especially among Anglicans and Lutherans but not only there, insist that they are catholic; it is just that they are not Roman Catholic. I have considerable sympathy for that position, having insisted upon it myself for some thirty years. But, finally, being catholic is not a matter of being very catholic; it is a matter of being Catholic. Everything authentically catholic gravitates toward uppercase Catholic. Being catholic is a matter of one's theological position, historical consciousness, and sacramental sensibility; but, after all is said and done, it is also and necessarily a matter of what church one belongs to.

A Lutheran pastor and distinguished academic who was recently received into the Catholic Church wrote me: "Since I was a theological student I have considered myself a catholic Christian. Like you, I traveled under the banner called 'evangelical catholic.' In recent years, however, I began to realize that I was living in a church of my imagination." Newman, too, strove valiantly to convince himself and others that he belonged to a catholic church, only to be compelled to recognize that the Anglicanism of his theological imagination was "a paper church," that the only way to belong to a catholic church is to belong to the Catholic Church. Some churches are in important ways more catholic than others, but the Catholic Church is the Catholic Church. At least that is the claim, and everything turns on whether it is true.

A great strength of *Lead, Kindly Light* is that the author does not blink at all that is unsatisfactory in the Catholic Church today. There is so much that is unsatisfactory; there always has been and there always will be until the final coming of the promised Kingdom of God. I confess to missing the more elevated liturgical language and, most painfully, the great hymnody that I knew as a Lutheran. Dr. Howard has his own list of thoroughly justified discontents with contemporary Catholicism. But all that fades into relative insignificance by comparison with all that is gained in becoming a Catholic. In any event, the point is not whether I prefer being a Catholic, although I do. The point, as Thomas Howard rightly insists, is "whether something is true or not."

RICHARD JOHN NEUHAUS

1

On Being Branded an Expatriate

To move from one religious neighborhood to another is to lay oneself open to all sorts of speculations from the bystanders. "He was swept away emotionally"—this if one has made one's move in the flush of ardor that suffuses various revivalist options, say; or "He was looking for a dignity and sublimity in worship that seemed missing in his erstwhile world"—this if one goes from a rustic conventicle to one of the liturgical churches, most especially the Anglicanism that is so often borne to us on the thin notes echoing amongst the arches of the chapel at King's College, Cambridge; or "He was the type who needed authority"—this if one becomes a Catholic.

There is often a great deal of truth in these remarks. Indeed, one may have been swept away, or may have yearned for sublimity, or have looked earnestly for authority. But to point that out is to leave unasked, much less unanswered, the question as to whether the move was ill-conceived, or was at bottom made in obedience to light having been cast on one's itinerary. It is impossible, of course, to settle that question simply on the apparent merits of the case itself. The bystanders, most of them, will judge the matter according to views which they already hold, and go on about their business. A few may be bemused enough to undertake some scrutiny of their own notions.

At the age of fifty I was received into the holy Catholic Church. The move occurred at the hither end of an itinerary which had begun for me in the trusty Protestant Fundamentalism of the nineteen-thirties and forties, and had taken me thence through Anglicanism, and eventually to the threshold of the "one, holy, catholic, and apostolic Church." Such a sequence is far from being unprecedented: Cardinal Manning and Cardinal Newman, in the nineteenth century, followed not altogether dissimilar routes, and Monsignor Ronald Knox, in our own century. To adduce these worthies is to place oneself in company so august that any analogy between one's own pilgrimage and theirs seems grotesque. I would only venture the point that dwarfs *can* follow in the footsteps of giants, albeit laboriously.

2

My Roots

I say the Fundamentalism which formed my religious nurture was "trusty." By that I would wish to distinguish it from the various manifestations of popular salvationism and biblical literalism that often decline into tatterdemalion customs and manners. We all have images of shouting, sweating stump preachers, or of ropy-necked women with their hair skinned back into a knot, bawling hymns on street corners to the accompaniment of harmoniums and tambourines, or of Sunday night chapels in dingy streets where the lower classes clap their hands, wave their arms, and kneel at the rail to roar prayers into the ears of heaven.

These are caricatures to be attributed mostly to cinema and the stage. If there is any truth in these pictures, then the Fundamentalism of my youth would have to be distinguished from them. The believers in my world were certainly drawn from the "not many mighty" of this world; and good taste, when it came to the melodies and sentiments that turned up in the hymnody, and the general manner of speaking of things divine, was scarcely one of its strong points. But there was a clarity—a transparency even—and a forthrightness and muscularity in these people's way of holding the Faith that often elude the experience of people in more soberly-tailored regions of Christendom. They talked, sometimes gabbled, about "the Lord," and they laced their exchanges with tags from Scripture ("Well, Jehovah Jireh!" or "Maranatha!"), and were much given to volunteering their "testimony," meaning thereby that they would relate for you how they had got saved, and how the Lord had led them in this way and that.

I myself am not disposed to scoff in this connection. Questions of style are vexed questions, and to thread one's way along in such a topic and say much to the purpose is very difficult. The ardor and simplicity of people whose religious taste might embarrass oneself may well exist on a far higher plane than one's own reticence and fastidiousness.

It was our father and mother who furnished the particular cast, or hue, which characterized the religion in the house where I and my five brothers and sisters grew up. We received from them a notably "civilized," or well-mannered, rendering of the Faith. Both of my parents were from old Philadelphia, with all that this implies of reticence, polite self-effacement, and well-schooled gentility. They shared, unabashedly, the confidence in Holy Scripture that has always marked Protestant Fundamentalism, and they taught us the Christian Faith in such a way that we held it as an intensely vibrant, personal thing. They prayed with us twice daily at family prayers and again at our bedside at night. We sang hymns—hundreds of them—learning them all by heart, and heard our father sing them into the mirror while he shaved ("If I Gained the World but Lost the Saviour," or "I Will Sing the Wondrous Story of the Christ Who Died for Me"), and whistle them up and down the stairs, and play them on the piano at odd moments of the day. "The Lord" was at one's elbow unflaggingly, which was both a great solace, in that he knew one's fears and griefs, and a restraint from evil, since he knew everything one was thinking and muttering. This awareness tended to keep us back from the grosser expressions of rage or frustration—or at least audible renderings. Christians in our quarter really did not swear in those days, and the lush profanity of our Catholic friends made us feel that they were not Christians at all. Christians didn't swear. We also did not dance or smoke or go to the cinema or drink wine or gamble. Our Catholic friends indulged in every single one of these activities with the greatest insouciance: they could not possibly have been Christians.

The family next door was Catholic. Their two sons were my playmates and friends until I went away to school at fifteen. Looking back now, from the perspective of fifty years, I can see that this was a household in which one might see, in a particularly faithful rendering, just what Catholicism can look like in ordinary lay life. Weekly Mass (the whole family loaded into the green 1940 Ford), the rosary, various statues at strategic points in the house, the Baltimore Catechism, Sacred Heart schooling for the daughter—it was all there. But I did not think of them as *Christians*. To earn that label, one had to use a highly particular phraseology in connection with matters religious, and, beyond that, one had to be much more loquacious about the Faith than these people were. Besides, both the father and mother smoked, and one could see playing cards and gin bottles about in the house, so one knew that they couldn't quite be Christian. (On the other hand, my mother and their mother often had long chats about Christianity—my mother "witnessing" to her—and I can remember that my mother's conclusion was that they were, in fact, believers after all. They just had so much *else* going.)

The town where we lived was a Quaker town, and Quakerism was still in the air. The cool, quiet, streets shaded with huge oaks and maples, the stately houses, the two Friends' Meeting Houses, and the thee's and thou's which one heard daily: it was a decorous and gracious ambiance. Various newer elements had arrived (us and the Catholics), and it seemed that there were now more Fitzgeralds, McChesneys, and O'Donnells than there were Stokeses and Lippincotts. I had a paper route, and I had to go every afternoon to a shack on Second Street (*not* one of your Quaker streets) to pick up my bundle of papers. Most of the other paperboys were Catholics, and the talk was ribald in the extreme. I can remember my astonishment, then, when one of them rattled off the Apostles' Creed one day. *"He* knows *that?"* I wondered. He seemed to assume that it was all true, too. Up on Main Street one saw nuns, walking two by two, now and again. There was a convent next to the big stone Church of Our Lady of Good Counsel. The last word in the name of the parish was chiseled in the stone as "Covnsel," and this used to divert me endlessly. The nuns had tall headdresses, high black leather lace-up shoes that one could just glimpse as they swished along, and vastly complicated strings of black beads hanging down their skirts. Most of them seemed to wear rimless hexagonal glasses whose bows disappeared back into their starched wimples. I was always made anxious if I had to pass them for fear they would discover something wrong about me and seize me by the hair (one heard many tales from the children who went to the parochial school). There was a girl named Elizabeth Barrett in my class at our school, whom I knew to be Catholic. She used to speak of "Our Lord" once in a while. There must be something wrong about that, I thought: one says "*The* Lord." But she seemed to be wholehearted in both the naturalness and the reverence with which she spoke this title. How it was that she could *not* be a Christian, I was not entirely sure. (Besides, she had the courage to speak of Jesus, whereas I, who had a corner on access to him, could never muster any such courage. My Sunday school had given us little red pins saying "Jesus Saves" on them, as openers for witnessing. "Did he save you?" asked a boy named Donny Flynn one day. "No," said I, and that was the end of my efforts at witnessing. I took the pin off on the spot.)

My father and mother did not speak disparagingly of Catholics however, only pointing out to us what they thought was a vast and top-heavy superstructure that Rome had built over "the simplicity that is in Christ." Rosaries, penances, rote prayers, statues, holy cards, novenas, the Virgin, the saints, compulsory attendance at Mass, salvation by works: somehow, they said, the "gospel" had got obscured. "Believe on the Lord Jesus Christ and thou shalt be saved": Catholics did not seem to attach much weight to St. Paul's words to the Philippian jailer, if indeed they had even come across them. (That was another thing: Catholics didn't read the Bible.) "Ye must be born again" was how the Lord himself condensed the gospel for Nicodemus; but Catholics did not appear to know what the injunction might mean, at least on any conscious, practical level.

The Fundamentalism of my youth, then, inculcated in me and my brothers and sisters, and in all good Fundamentalists, a piety arising directly from the text of the Bible—from the very phraseology of the King James Bible, actually—and almost wholly shaped by this stress on the text. Not only were Noah and Abraham and Moses and David familiar figures; we also knew Caleb and Achan and Gehazi and Abner intimately. We could find the Minor Prophets —Haggai or Nahum—in a flash, as well as the tiny epistles of John and Jude. We could quote perhaps hundreds of verses from both testaments, and we tried to configure our spiritual lives in the light of St. Paul's teachings, especially in Romans, Galatians, Ephesians, and Philippians. The Gospels, oddly enough, were tacitly de-emphasized in those days, very probably because the Fundamentalists sensed (quite correctly) that the modernists, under Harnack and Renan and Schleiermacher, and most recently Harry Emerson Fosdick, had whittled down the Christian Faith to a matter of emulating the Nazarene, and had jettisoned quite categorically the apostolic preaching on human sinfulness, repentance, and salvation through the sacrifice on the Cross. "The Blood" was *the* test in those days: the modernists cordially detested this gospel of the bleeding Lamb of God, and the Fundamentalists hammered it home.

We were taught to read the Bible daily in private, and to pray extemporaneously. By the time adolescence arrived we were engaged in a sustained and assiduous program of personal spiritual discipline, attempting to keep ourselves under the scrutiny of Scripture—"Thy word have I hid in my heart, that I might not sin against thee," or "If ye through the spirit do mortify the deeds of the body, ye shall live," or "Rejoicing in hope, patient in tribulation," and so forth—

and praying that God would "show us his will for our lives," which most probably meant jungle missions service.

To this energetic school of piety, taught to me principally by my parents, but also in church and at the boarding school and college where I and my brothers and sisters all went, I would attribute my early and lasting sense of the *earnestness* of the Faith. Until the hour of my death (and, I hope, beyond that) I will feel myself to be addressed directly, as it were, by the Lord. Fundamentalism, I felt, did away, quite summarily, with the notion of Christianity as "my religion," and brought me into the precincts where I stood alone and naked before God. The idea of "my religion" introduced a note of arbitrariness into the matter, and interposed something (a set of practices, say) between me and God, who was right there looking at me.

I say the "earnestness" of the Faith. There is nothing cavalier about Fundamentalist piety. You cannot toy with morals, for example, and Fundamentalists are put off their stride by the way some Episcopalians, say, love to joke about holy things, crossing themselves and rolling their eyes over an apparent sacrilege, or shuddering with scandalized delight at how much incense this or that extreme parish uses. This earnestness has its pharisaic side; but I would guess that the round-eyed solemnity with which I tend to approach Catholicism now was planted in my sensibilities by Fundamentalism. Certainly the profoundly Christocentric orientation of my faith, and the immediacy which I attach to Scripture, along with my unmingled confidence in it, and my disposition to venerate the great lineage of the faithful from "righteous Abel" down to John Paul II, and the huge moral weight which invests the Faith for me, may all be seen as having had their planting and early nourishment in Fundamentalism.

3

A Step toward Rome

When I was twenty-five or so, I was received into the Anglican Church. There had lurked on the borders of my imagination ever since my early childhood an almost fathomless yearning for—for what? I was not sure. Beauty? Ancient hymnody? The ineffable? Storied windows richly dight, casting a dim religious light? Polyphony? Liturgy? I scarcely knew. But the Anglican (Episcopal) Church, with its (then) Elizabethan Prayer Book and its Gothic buildings and its ritual and ceremony and seraphic music, presented itself as the keeper of the thing I sought.

I felt that I had found "it" in this four hundred-year-old church. Indeed, I found more than I had known to wish for. The hymns, for one thing, opened out onto vistas at once glorious and mysterious: "O Food of Men Wayfaring," and "Christ, the Fair Glory of the Holy Angels," and "Deck Thyself, My Soul, with Gladness," and "O, What Their Joy and Their Glory Must

Be"—we felt we were surrounded with aeonian throngs of saints and angels as we sang. And the "Te Deum," evoking "the glorious company of the apostles, the goodly fellowship of the prophets, the noble army of martyrs," drew us into precincts of insupportable felicity. The prose of the Prayer Book—"O God, forasmuch as without Thee . . ." and "Vouchsafe, O Lord . . ." and "Whose service is perfect freedom"— seemed the very language of heaven itself. I heard the great Renaissance Masses of Tomás Luis de Victoria, Josquin, Byrd, and Palestrina sung with that breathy "white" treble of the English cathedral choir, wholly without vibrato, so different from the warblings of satin-robed middle-aged Protestant choirs. The mysterious amalgam of humility and great dignity which is the particular hallmark of the Anglican liturgy ("We do not presume to come to this Thy Table, O merciful Lord, trusting in our own righteousness, but in Thy manifold and great mercies...") —this disclosed to me a hitherto unknown posture before the *Mysterium Tremendum.* Indeed, who had so much as heard tell of the *Mysterium Tremendum?*

For twenty-five years I worshipped and lived as an Anglican, and during that time I came to see that the Eucharistic liturgy, far from being merely "a" worship service among many options all spread out like a smorgasbord to please the sundry tastes of us Christians, was "the prayer of the Church," the Great Thanksgiving, which took shape very quickly after Pentecost, and constituted, quite simply, what the ancient Church had understood by worship. It is not a disputed point: the denominations that have substituted a "worship service" with the sermon as the *pièce de resistance,* only intermittently including "communion," would agree that yes, they have, in fact, substituted a recently-devised service for the Church's ancient Eucharistic liturgy, but that they have good reasons for doing so.

One line of argument on this point invokes differing tastes as the rationale for variety in worship: some folks like banjos (goes this line of thought), and some like polyphony, and some like handclapping, or songs projected onto a movie screen, or spontaneity, or incense, or whatever. It's all a matter of what one prefers. *Chacun à son goût.*

This is a confused line of thought. The Church, as she moved out into the long haul of history during the decades that followed Pentecost, did not cobble up varieties of "worship experiences" in response to what everybody wanted. Liturgy is not just a fancy service for people who like ritual: it is "the work of the people" (that is what the word means), and that work, from the beginning, has been understood by the Church to be the offering of our worship in union with Christ's self-offering to the Father. The Lord's Table is the particular locale of this offering of ours. The modern preaching service abbreviates the liturgy, lopping off the *Anaphora* (the Offering—that is, the Eucharist itself) and leaving only the *Synaxis* (the "gathering"—that is, the readings from Scripture and the homily).

I also became accustomed to the Church year as an Anglican. Fundamentalism had taught me the Scriptures, and had thereby familiarized me with all of the events attending upon our redemption: the Annunciation, the Nativity, the Crucifixion, and so on. But one's own piety had no corresponding shape, or sequence, as it were, and neither did the 365 days of the calendar for the congregation. One could embark on one's own private reading of Judges, or Luke, or Second Corinthians in April, perhaps, and pursue this for as many weeks as one felt was fruitful. It was one's own choice; and it was not a bad scheme. Or the pastor could institute a twenty-week series on "Law and Grace," or on the Book of Romans, or on "Old Testament Women of Faith" in February, and then start a new series on the prophets in July. There was no recurrent "shape" for personal or congregational piety mediated by a Church year. In those days we observed Christmas and Easter and no more— not even Good Friday, if I remember correctly. Each had its place on one day in the year—with no preparation and no octave following—and the next Sunday we would continue with our study of Job or the like.

It was, therefore, a discovery to me to find that from time almost immemorial the Christian Church has followed a rich and disciplined sequence in her yearly calendar, beginning with Advent and concluding with the long season of Pentecost, which brings the faithful around to Advent once again. To move with hundreds of millions of fellow-Christians through this recurrent pattern is to move pensively and joyously through the sequence of the gospel itself as it was enacted for us on the stage of our earthly history. It is to take one's place with Suzanna and Joanna, and Martha, and Peter and Andrew and Nicodemus and Joseph of Arimathea, as these followers and onlookers stumbled along near the Savior as he moved through the events that constitute our salvation. All of us, whether we find ourselves in one of the so-called "free" churches which have no liturgy or church year, or in one of the ancient liturgical churches, want to draw near to these events in our innermost being; but left to the fits and starts of our own resolves and schemes, as often as not we find that we are mired in a higgledy-piggledy business. How much better it is to hand the immense task over to the venerable wisdom of the Church herself, so that the pattern of our interior life takes shape as a matter of obedience and not of our own devising.

I also discovered, while I was an Anglican, that the Church year is studded with days on which we mark and recall the lives and, not infrequently, the martyr's deaths of the faithful who have gone ahead of us in The Way, and who exhibit to us noteworthy sanctity, intrepidity, fidelity, or wisdom. These are the so-called saints' days. Since we are creatures whose thoughts are both influenced and fed from a thousand sources—television, cinema, journals, books, fashions, conversation—we should leap at and prize the chance offered to us by the Church to turn our thoughts, if only briefly, to figures who show to us in the bright colors of actual human life what it is to be numbered among the faithful. Matthew, Barnabas, Felicity and Perpetua, Athanasius, Martin, Hildegard, Charles Borromeo, Teresa, John Vianney. What images fill my imagination: Elizabeth Taylor? Michael Jackson? Senator Kennedy? Compelling images all. From which ones will I draw my cues?

I think that, along with the Eucharistic liturgy and the Church year, the third contribution which the Anglicans made to my preparation for Catholicism was in the matter of the sacraments.

It is possible to be a Christian believer quite eager to insist upon the literal, physical aspect which our salvation took on when it broke into our history on this earth: a real birth (from a virgin, forsooth) and infancy; a body on a cross which "bore" our wickedness; that body dead and risen again, and taken into the Holy Trinity—it is possible to espouse all of this "physicality" with the greatest zeal, and yet to have one's piety altogether devoid of the physical. Manicheanism (the effort to expunge the physical from one's religion so that one is left with a purely disembodied "spiritual" remainder)—Manicheanism has always breathed down the neck of well-meaning Christian believers. One wants to be spiritual. "Reality is invisible, after all. God dwells not in temples made with hands. It is the spirit that quickeneth: the flesh profiteth nothing." It is easy enough to see how a person could arrive at the notion that Christianity is a strictly spiritual (meaning, in this context, non-material) affair. But no, says the Church. Our salvation, far from entailing an escape from the physical into a vacuous religious ether, entailed an Incarnation, physical agony, and resurrection, and it redeems the whole man, body, soul, and spirit. The apostles baptized their converts in water, in obedience to explicit instructions from the Lord himself. New birth was not to be sundered from the water of baptism: this is a sundering unknown and unimagined in the New Testament. And the faithful were to be fed with the very Flesh and Blood of the Savior: the Church from the beginning took Christ's words in the sixth chapter of John's Gospel very solemnly.

The Anglican Church introduced me to this "seamless" sacramental vision of things, that is, to the understanding that we do not live in a starkly double-decker universe, with matter on a low level and spirit higher up. The important divisions for the Christian Faith are the divisions not between matter and spirit but rather, first, between Creator and Creation, with the latter category comprising everything made, from the "spiritual" (i.e., non-physical) seraphim down to flatworms and slime molds and shale; and second, between Good and Evil, with Evil comprising anything, from Lucifer (spirit) on down to my own sullenness, pusillanimity and niggardliness, with suffering, death, and hell included—anything, that is, which stands in rebellion against the Most High. There is no physical *thing* which is, in itself, evil: there is only the wrong *use* of things (say, the body for adultery, or wine in excess, or gold for avarice), or the infecting, polluting, and ruination of things (disease, decay, death) as a tragic byproduct of evil.

For as long as (fallen) history lasts, the sacraments stand as a perpetual pledge of the reknitting of the fabric of Creation, so sadly torn apart by us in our act of rebellion in Eden. The pelts of the animals sacrificed by God for the covering of our shame constituted the opening gambit in the long sequence that took us through altars and blood and burned fat, and incense and gold and acacia wood, right up to the Annunciation, when Salvation itself came upon us, not as mere edict, decree, or law from heaven, but in our flesh—physically.

The Anglican Church, with the ancient Orthodox and Catholic Churches, is a sacramentalist church to which salvation is more than propositional. The preaching of the Word occurs most characteristically in union with the sacramental Word—the Word-made-flesh, "made present" (this is what *anamnesis,* the word the Lord used for "remembrance," means), in the Eucharist.

4

The Church's Roots

During my twenty-five years as an Anglican I found myself reading. As I read, year after year, I became intrigued, and then bothered, and finally hag-ridden by the question "What is the Church?"

Every Sunday at the Anglican liturgy I found myself repeating, "I believe in one, holy, catholic, and apostolic Church." These are words from an era which all of us—Catholic, Orthodox, Anglican, Protestant, and unaffiliated—must take seriously, since all of us, whether we are pleased to admit it or not, are the direct beneficiaries of the work of the men who hammered out those words. Not a few of us may think, during our less reflective moments, that all we need is the Bible and our own wits. *Sola Scriptura.* Just me and my Bible. But that is a notion unimaginable to the ancient Church. Every Christian in every assembly of believers in this world is incalculably in the debt of the men who succeeded the apostles. For they are the ones who, during those early centuries when the Church was moving from the morning of Pentecost out into the long haul of history, fought and thought and worked and wrote, and died, so that "the faith once for all delivered to the saints" might indeed be handed on. Heresiarchs popped up out of the weeds left, right, and center, and all of them believed in the "verbal inspiration" of Scripture. It was the Church, in her bishops and councils, that preserved the Faith from the errors of the heresiarchs and other zealots, and that shepherded the faithful along in The Way.

As an Anglican I felt that I was in some sense "catholic," but I was unhappy that the church to which I had given my allegiance was reluctant to speak authoritatively, *as a church,* on just what we, the laity, were to believe. This was a state of affairs that would have been unimaginable to our Fathers in the Faith in the early days of the Church. That is, whereas in apostolic and patristic times the faithful could look to their bishops to clarify and settle for them the various points that blew into the air—about the mystery of Christ, or the Trinity, or baptism, say—we were all at odds when it came to deciding such points. For example, I knew that whereas many—most?—Anglicans believed that the bread and wine in the Eucharist were in some sense "sacramental" and therefore that there was a mystery at work, thousands of Anglicans went much further and insisted, with Rome, on the doctrine of transubstantiation. And even though the Articles of Religion in their Prayer Book spoke on the matter, mutually exclusive views were held and taught in seminaries. Or again, on baptism: the Prayer Book uses the word "regenerate" in connection with the rite, but thousands of "low church" Anglicans demurred, and skirted the doctrine, stressing a conscious transaction of faith when they spoke about regeneration. As a church, we were all at odds when it came to deciding just what was to be believed on many points. This state of affairs was exacerbated almost immeasurably in the "free" churches from which I had come as a Fundamentalist. Oh, to be sure, we all agreed on the so-called "fundamentals" of the gospel—but, I learned, those fundamentals had been articulated and distilled for us *by the Church* which wrote the creeds. The Mormons and the Jehovah's Witnesses and the modernists, whom we would have excluded from the pale of the Faith, all toiled away at the pages of the Bible itself, but we would have said that they were not getting the same things *out of* that Bible.

Why did we say that, I wondered? Because (the answer came), whether we acknowledged it or not, our "orthodox" understanding of the

Bible had been articulated for us by the Church. Almost overnight after Pentecost all sorts of notions had cropped up which the Church rejected as not in harmony with the Faith delivered by the apostles; and the reason we are not now Nestorians nor Eutychians nor Apollinarians nor Docetists nor Arians nor Montanists is that *the Church* received and guarded and interpreted and taught the Bible, and we the faithful have had a reliable and apostolic voice in the Church that says, *"This* is what Holy Scripture is to be understood as teaching; and *that* which you hear Eutychius or Sabellius teaching from the Bible (they say) is not to be believed."

When I heard myself repeating the words from the Nicene Creed, at the Anglican liturgy, "I believe in one, holy, catholic, and apostolic Church," I knew I was saying words that are not directly from any one text in the Bible, and yet that have been spoken in all of Christendom for a millennium and a half now, constituting a plumb-line for us. The Creed is not Scripture; that is true. But then all of us, whether we come from groups which repeat the Creed or not, would agree, "Oh yes, indeed: that is the Faith which we all profess." A few would add, "But, of course, we get it straight out of the Bible. We don't need any creed."

The great difficulty here, as it were, was that Eutychius and Sabellius and Arius got *their* notions straight out of the Bible as well. Who will arbitrate these things for us? Who will speak with authority to us faithful, all of us rushing about flapping the pages of our well-thumbed New Testaments, locked in shrill contests over the two natures of Christ, or baptism, or the Lord's Supper, or the mystery of predestination?

This question formed itself in the following way for me, a twentieth-century Protestant (and again, as an Anglican, I *hoped* that in some sense I was "catholic," but one thing was certain: I did not need to listen to the Apostolic See in Rome on matters of dogma or morals; to this extent, then, I was most certainly Protestant): Who will arbitrate for us all between Luther and Calvin on the weighty matters that lie between those two teachers? And who will tell us whether to believe Luther or Zwingli when it comes to the Lord's Supper, since either the bread and wine are or are not Christ's Body and Blood, and there is no convenient middle ground on the point? And who will arbitrate for us between George Whitefield and John Wesley, both Anglican divines, and each preaching a doctrine of salvation that excludes the other's teaching categorically (that is, either Christ died for everybody, or he died only for the elect)? And who will decide for us between all the Protestant churches and Mr. J. N. Darby who, in the early nineteenth century, started up the Plymouth Brethren on the notion that *all* the churches were wrong about how the Lord's followers were to gather? And who will decide for us laity between the Dispensationalists (who have worked out the Last Things to the smallest scintilla) and the Calvinists (who reject the Dispensationalists' teaching out of hand)?

A particularly piquant, not to say painful, version of this jumble presented itself to us Anglicans and Fundamentalists—especially the latter, with whom I still felt myself to be deeply connected—when a critical issue like sexual morality arose. The Anglican bishops are curiously reluctant to pronounce on touchy issues with any language other than tergiversation. And the Fundamentalists, while they may have fierce and exact views, all have their own spheres of influence—independent congregations and affiliations and seminaries—so that no one needs to listen to anyone else. Who will speak to us, the believing laity, I wondered, with any authority? I must confess that in my truculent moods I was tempted to tweak the noses of my Protestant brothers by telling them (not altogether fancifully, actually) that the best they could do in the face of touchy issues like sex was to run a symposium in one of their journals (to whose editorial policy no one was bound to conform his ideas), with one article by a traditionalist theologian and one by, say, a lesbian feminist, with the former plumping for traditional under-standings of the Bible, and the latter showing, with virtuoso hermeneutic derring-do, that we have all been wrong for the entire thirty-five hundred years since Sinai, that what the Bible really teaches is that homosexuals, for example, may enjoy fully-expressed and active sexual lives.

The trouble there, for me, was that unlike the apostolic Church we non-Catholics had no desk where the buck stopped. Scripture clearly did not constitute such a desk, since, for one thing, both parties to all disputes always ap-pealed energetically to Scripture; and second, St. Paul had called the *Church,* not the Bible, "the pillar and ground of the truth" (1 Tm 3.15).

Protestantism was not, whatever else I might have wished to say about it, a picture of things that would have been at all recognizable to the apostles, nor to the generations which followed them. The faithful from Pentecost on were cer-tainly aware of a great babel of voices among the Christians, teaching this and teaching that, on every conceivable point of revelation. But the faithful were also aware that there was a body that could speak into the chaos and declare with serene and final authority what the Faith that had been taught by the apostles *was*. Clearly we modern non-Catholics were living in a scheme of things altogether unimaginable to the Twelve Apostles and the Fathers of the Church.

"I believe in one, holy, catholic, and apostolic Church," I found myself saying in the Creed. What Church? What *is* the Church? What was the Church in the minds of the men who framed that Creed? Clearly it was not the donnybrook that the world sees nowadays, with literally thousands of groups, big and small, all clamoring and all claiming to be, in one sense or another, the Church.

I became aware that I, as an individual believer, stood in a very long and august lineage of the faithful, stretching back to the apostles and fathers. The picture had changed for me: it was no longer primarily me, my Bible, and Jesus (although heaven knows that is not altogether a bad picture: the only question is, is it the *whole* picture?). Looming for me, as an Anglican, was "the Faith," ancient, serene, undimmed, true. And that Faith could not be split apart from the Church. But then what was the Church?

5

Ecclesiastical Confrontation

I realized that, one way or another, I had to come to terms with the Church in all of its antiquity, its authority, its unity, its liturgy, and its sacraments. These five marks, or aspects, of the Church were matters which all of us non-Catholics would find to be eluding us.

First, the antiquity of the Church confronts me. As an Anglican I wanted to see myself as obedient to this ancient Church. But why were we not in obedience, or communion, with that Church as it has understood itself, apparently, for nearly two thousand years? Something had introduced a fissure between us in Canterbury and the Apostolic See in Rome, and the mixture of Henry VIII's sins and highhandedness with Reformation doctrines, to my mind, did not constitute a footing from which one should launch a new church. Whatever could be said about Anglicanism's still having the apostolic succession, we were manifestly out of communion with the See which had constituted the touchstone of catholic identity for all Christians for more than a millennium before the sixteenth century (and still did for nine hundred million of my fellow-Christians).

As a Fundamentalist I had discovered while I was in college that it is possible to dismiss the entire Church as having gone off the rails by about AD 95. That is, we, with our open Bibles, knew better than did old Ignatius or Clement, who had been taught by the very apostles themselves, just what the Church is and what it should look like. Never mind that our worship services would have been unrecognizable to them, or that our governance would have been equally unrecognizable: we were right, and the fathers were wrong (about bishops, and about the Eucharist). That settled the matter.

The trouble here, for me, was that what these wrong-headed men wrote—about God, about our Lord Jesus Christ, about his Church, about the Christian's walk and warfare—was so titanic, and so rich and so luminous, that their error seemed infinitely truer and more glorious than my truth. I gradually felt that it was I, not they, who was under surveillance. The "glorious company of the apostles, the noble army of martyrs, and the holy Church throughout all the world" (to quote the ancient hymn, the "Te Deum") judge *me,* not I them. Ignatius, Polycarp, Clement, Justin, Irenaeus, Cyprian, Cyril, Basil, the Gregorys, Augustine, Ambrose, Hilary, Benedict—it is under the gaze of this senate that I find myself standing. Alas. How tawdry, how otiose, how flimsy, how embarrassing seem the arguments that I had been prepared so gaily to put forward against the crushing radiance of these men's confessions.

The Church is here, in all of its antiquity, judging me.

Second, the Church in its authority confronts me. That strange authority to bind and loose which our Lord bestowed on his disciples, recorded in Matthew 16 and 18, has not evaporated from the Church—or so the Church has believed from the beginning. If one will read the story of those decades which followed Pentecost, and especially that followed upon the death of the apostles, one will discover that the unction to teach and to preside in the Church that passed from the Lord to the apostles, and from the apostles to the bishops, was understood to be an apostolic unction. I, for example, could not start up out of the bulrushes and say, "Hi, everybody! The Lord has led me to be a bishop! I'm starting me a church over here."

The whole Christian community—bishop, presbyters, deacons, and laity—would have looked gravely at me and gone on about their business. The Holy Spirit, in those days, did not carry on private transactions with isolated souls, and then announce to the Church that so-and-so had been anointed for this or that ministry. Even in the extreme case of Paul, the Damascus Road crisis had to be subjected to and ratified by the Church. The unction of the Holy Spirit and the authority of the Church to ordain for ministry were not two random enterprises. The Holy Spirit chose to work in and through the Church's ministry and voice. To be sure, he could have done anything he wanted to do, being God. Under the Old Covenant he chose to work in and through Israel; though one does find extra characters like Job and Jethro and Melchizedek and the Magi coming across the stage from outside the Covenant, yet nonetheless undeniably having been in touch with God. God can do what he wants.

But the Church down through the centuries has understood herself to be the appointed vessel for God's working, in the ordinary run of things. Her authority is not her own. She arrogates nothing to herself. Her bishops are the merest custodians, the merest passers-on, we might say, of the Deposit of Faith. As a Roman Catholic now, I am acutely conscious of this. When someone objects to me, "But who does the Catholic Church think she is, taking this high and mighty line?" (about abortion, say, or about sexual morality, or about who may or may not come to the Lord's Table), the answer is, "She doesn't think she is anyone in particular, if you mean that she has set herself up among the wares in the flea market as somehow the best. She has her given task to do—to pass on the teaching given by the apostles—and she has no warrant to change that. She is not taking her cues from the Nielsen ratings, nor from a poll, nor even from a sociological survey as to what people feel comfortable with nowadays. *She* didn't start the Church, and it's not her Church."

As a free-church Christian, and even as an Anglican, one can make up one's own mind about many things. Shall I fast or not? Well, that's for me to decide. Shall I give alms? Again—a matter for my own judgment. Must I go to church? That, certainly, is my own affair. Need I observe this or that holy day in the calendar? I will decide. Piety and devotion and discipline are matters of one's own tailoring: no one may peer over my shoulder and tell me what to do.

And, indeed, no one may do any such thing—*if* we are speaking of ourselves as Americans who have constitutional rights. But if we are speaking of ourselves as Christian believers, then there is a touchstone other than the Constitution by which our choices must be tested. Our Christian ancestors knew nothing of this sprightly individualism when it came to the disciplines of the Christian life. Things took shape in the Church very early; and nobody dreamed of cobbling up a wholly private and independent spirituality and discipline.

This recognition of the Church as having authority to speak in such matters carried over into bigger questions. Shall women be ordained as priests? It is, eventually, not a matter of job description, nor of politics, nor of rights, nor even of common sense or public justice. The question is settled by what the Church understands the priesthood to be. It is not a question to be left interminably open in the public forum for decade after decade of hot debate.

The Church is here, in all of its authority, judging me.

Third, the Church in its unity confronts me. This was a most difficult and daunting matter. But one thing was becoming inexorably clear: my erstwhile and happy idea of the Church's unity as being nothing more than the worldwide clutter that we (especially we Fundamentalists) have under our general umbrella was not what the ancient Church had understood by this word "unity." As a free-church Christian, and even to a certain extent as an Anglican, I could pick and choose which source of things appealed most to me: this writer or that one; this seminary or that one; this school of theology or that one; this charismatic leader or that one. Variety is doubtless a sign of vigorous life in the Church, and the Catholic Church has always exhibited a most exuberant variety: Augustine and Aquinas; Francis and Dominic; Spain and Ireland; Poland and France; Mexico and England; Benedictine and baroque; Charlemagne and Brother Charles of Jesus. A great, leaping, coruscating rondo, so to speak.

But variety becomes disastrous if I invest any of the above with the authority that belongs alone to the Church. But then who shall guide my choices?

Once again I found myself driven back to the understanding of things at work in the ancient Church. Whatever varieties of expression there may have been—in Alexandria as over against Lyons, or in Antioch as over against Rome—when it came to the Faith itself, and also to order and discipline and piety in the Church, no one was left groping or mulling over the choices in the flea market. Where we (non-Catholics) were pleased to live with a muddle, and even with stark contradictions (Luther vs. Zwingli, for example, on the Lord's Supper), the Church of antiquity was united. No one needed to remain in doubt forever as to what the Church might be, or where it might be found.

The Montanists in the early Church were certainly zealous and earnest, and had much to commend them: the difficulty, finally, was that they were *not the Church*. Likewise with the Donatists: God bless them for their fidelity and ardor and purity; but they were *not the Church*. Or, as protracted and difficult as the Arian controversy was, no one needed to remain forever in doubt as to what the Church had settled upon: Athanasius fought for the *Church* against *heresy*. The question was closed. There was one Church: the Church was one. And this was a discernible, visible, embodied unity, not a loose aggregate of moderately like-minded believers with their various task forces all across the globe. The bishop of Antioch was not analogous to the General Secretary of the World Evangelical Fellowship, nor to the head of the National Association of Evangelicals (these are bona fide organizations, not hypothetical bodies introduced here for purposes of the argument). He could speak with the full authority of the Church behind him, whereas these latter gentlemen can only speak for their own organizations. The bishop was not even analogous to the Stated Clerk of the Presbyterian Church, nor the Presiding Bishop of the Episcopal Church, neither of whom is understood by his own clientele to be speaking in matters of doctrine and morals with an undoubted apostolic authority.

What is the unity of the Church? It is a question that has been answered too frivolously by too many believers since the Renaissance. I discovered that the Church early on began to look to the See of Rome, understood to be the See of Peter, as both the sign and the guarantor of the Church's unity here below, for as long as our human history lasts. *Of course* our Christian unity is in Christ, and to that extent we all hope that we will, all of us, Baptist and Copt, Mennonite and Maronite, lock arms and march into the lions' jaws, should such a day come, singing loudly, "Christ Is Made the Sure Foundation." But this Christ was *incarnate* in our history. Our union with him is, for as long as history lasts, localized, so to speak, and made visible and actual in physical terms—in the

Eucharist, that is. And thus it is with the Church—or so the Church Catholic has thought, from the beginning. Her unity is more than an idea or an ideal. Like all of these points at which the eternal touches time (the Annunciation, the Nativity, the Crucifixion), we find an invisible reality manifest in heavily physical terms. The Church is of one fabric with the whole gospel here: she is "invisible" in that only God knows, finally, where the outer hem of her skirt is; but she is visible in the form she has taken on in our mortal history, just as the Eternal Word became visible.

The Church is here, in its unity, judging me.

Fourth, the liturgy of the Church confronts and judges me. In what sense can anyone say that the liturgy "judges" him? Certainly it would not condemn a man or pass any explicit judgment on him.

But, if only by virtue of its extreme antiquity and universality, the liturgy constitutes a sort of touchstone for the whole topic of Christian worship. As an Anglican, as I have already averred, I had been initiated into the liturgical worship of the Church. Often the topic is approached, however, as though it were a matter of taste: John likes fancy worship—smells and bells—and Bill likes simplicity and spontaneity and informality—hymns projected onto a screen, perhaps, and time out for testimonials and unstructured praise. Certainly we must all admit that God does, mercifully, receive any effort, however halting and homespun, which anyone offers as worship, just as any father or mother will receive the offering of a limp fistful of dandelions as a nosegay from a tiny child. On the other hand, two considerations were borne in upon me during my years as an Anglican.

First, what did the Church from the beginning understand by worship—that is, by its corporate, regular act of worship? The book of Acts gives us little light on the precise shape or content of the Christians' gatherings: the apostles' doctrine, fellowship, the breaking of bread, and the prayers are mentioned. Saint Paul's epistles do not spell out what is to be done. We have to look to other early writings if we are curious about the apostolic Church's worship. And what we find when we do so is the Eucharistic liturgy. This, unmistakably, is what they did as worship. If we think we have improved on that pattern, I thought (looking backwards at my pre-Anglican days), we may wish to submit our innovations for scrutiny to the early Church in order to discover whether our innovations have, in fact, been improvements.

Which brings us to the second consideration: the content of the Eucharistic liturgy. From the beginning the Church has followed a given sequence when her people gathered to worship: first, readings from Scripture, the prayers, and preaching, and then, the so-called *Anaphora*— the "offering," or, as it came also to be called, the Great Thanksgiving. This was the great Eucharistic Prayer, which took on a fairly exact shape at the outset, and which you may still hear if you will listen to the liturgy in any of the ancient churches. Psalmody, canticle, and hymns also came to be included, and certain acclamations like the "Kyrie, eleison!" The whole presents a shape of such rich perfection that one wonders what exactly is the task of the "coordinators of worship" on the staff of various churches. The worship of the ancient Church is far from being a matter of endless tinkering, experimenting, and innovating. The entire mystery of revelation and redemption is unfurled for us in the Church's liturgy.

As an Anglican, I knew that we followed this liturgy—very often, apparently, with more punctilio and gravity than is to be found in many Catholic parishes. But I discovered that we were in a strange and indefinable position—almost a piggyback position liturgically, if such an undignified picture can at all be allowed in this sober context. That is, we admittedly owed the entirety of our worship to a tradition which, on the one hand, we celebrated, but from which, on the other, we kept ourselves aloof. We were *not Roman:* and yet we took our cues, old and new, from Rome. (This became noticeable in the revision of the liturgy in recent decades.) The liturgy, to put it another way, took shape over many centuries in a Church from which we wished to keep a delicate distance. We owed it to that ancient Church, and yet we insisted upon a very, very explicit distinction.

The Church's ancient liturgy is here, in all of its plenitude, majesty, and magnificence, judging me.

And lastly: the sacraments of the Church confront me. *Sacrament* is the Latin word for the Greek *mysterion,* mystery, or pledge. And, indeed, we are in the presence of mystery here, for the sacraments, like the Incarnation itself, constitute physical points at which the eternal touches time, or the unseen touches the seen, or grace touches nature. It is the Gnostics and Manicheans who want a purely disembodied religion. Anglicanism helped me greatly here.

Judaism and its fulfillment, Christianity, are heavy with matter, as it were. First we find creation itself, where solid matter was spoken into existence by the Word of God. Then redemption, beginning not with the wave of a spiritual wand, nor with mere edicts pronounced from the sky, but rather with skins and blood—the pelts of animals slaughtered by the Lord God to cover our guilty nakedness. Stone altars, blood, fat, scapegoats, incense, gold, acacia wood—the Old Covenant is heavily physical.

But then the New Covenant: we now escape into the purely spiritual and leave the physical behind, right? No. First a pregnancy and then a birth. Obstetrics and gynecology, right at the center of redemption. Fasting in the wilderness, water to wine, a crown of thorns, splinters and nails and blood—our eternal salvation achieved by grotesquely physical means.

But *then* pure spirituality, surely? No. A corpse resurrected; and then our human flesh taken up into the midmost mysteries of the eternal Godhead. Language itself staggers, and yet we affirm all of this. And bread and wine—Body and Blood—pledged and given to the Church for as long as history lasts.

In many quarters of Protestantism this great gift of the Eucharist has been huddled off to the periphery. This is understandable, since if you have a theology and a spirituality which stress the "inner" locale of piety, and understand salvation in terms of divine edicts, and say, *"Sola Scriptura,"* then naturally such unapologetically physical elements as bread and wine will fit only uneasily into the scheme. Anglicanism taught me the sacramentalist vision, as over against the more radical propositionalism of straight Protestantism: but Anglicanism itself speaks with an uncertain voice in this matter of the sacraments. One is free to be a Zwinglian (it is bread and wine, no more), or a transubstantiationalist, and still be an Anglican in good standing. It is a church unsure of something as fundamental as sacrament, and unwilling to speak clearly. This, by the way, is very far from being a taunt flung at Anglicanism by a nettled expatriate: Anglicanism glories consciously and explicitly in its *lack* of definition. She wears this quality as a cockade, not as a blot.

The Church's sacraments are here, with Christ, in their "scandalous" link with corporeality, judging me.

6

Deciding to Repatriate

But what form did all of this take in my own actual experience, it might be asked. What did you *do?*

A story like this is not easy to re-create accurately. Things happen in a random sort of way as often as not, and one's ideas, as they take shape and mature, do not yield themselves easily to an outline. When I look back I find that the line between my thoughts (the interior world) and what I did (the exterior world) is no longer altogether clear. Did I do thus and such because my thinking at that time obliged me to move? Or did I move only very tentatively and hesitantly, with my thoughts clarifying themselves after the fact? It is not always easy to recapture the picture.

But I can say this: By the summer of 1984 I had come up to the frontier of the Catholic Church—to the banks of the Tiber, to borrow a time-worn metaphor from other converts to

Rome down through the years. Sooner or later, mulling must give way to acting.

But what, exactly, is one to do? There is the rub, especially when one is fifty years old. Life-long Catholics probably have no inkling as to how a move into the ancient Church looms, terrifyingly, in the imagination of an about-to-be-convert. Such a move is as daunting as the decision to abandon one's citizenship and to be repatriated in a foreign country. It is one thing to make such a move if one has been only a nominal Christian anyway: the step into this or that denomination is only a matter of tech-nicalities. But if one has been a lifelong, deeply-committed Protestant, to make such a change is, in effect, to dismantle one's universe and step out into the unknown, or at least the very strange.

I did not "do" anything very brave or deci-sive, actually. I had been teaching at the summer session of a Protestant theological college in Vancouver, and at the end of the session, in mid-August, my wife and son flew to Vancouver from Boston to meet me, and to start south along the Pacific Coast, looking at the tourist attractions: San Francisco; the sequoias; Yosemite; the San Joaquin Valley; Carmel; Santa Barbara; Disneyland.

At Carmel one sunshiny morning we went into the Spanish mission of St. Charles Borromeo, founded in the seventeenth century by Blessed Junipero Serra. My memory is of stucco walls, ceramic tile roofs, cool interiors, bougainvillea—sumptuous bougainvillea—and flower gardens. For some reason—I have no recollection of being compelled by any great pressure—I stepped into a chapel where the Blessed Sacrament was reserved. (It appears in my memory as separate from the main church, but I cannot swear to this.) I remember kneeling down and, presently, saying, "Lead, kindly Light," borrowing the words from the hymn which John Henry Newman wrote when he was in a state of great indecision over this same question of the Church. I could not quite pray, "Make me a Catholic," since I did not really want to go that far. So I demurred with "Lead, kindly Light."

I am puzzled by this small vignette because I do not remember having been under a burden in this connection on that day. It was as though I were simply moving, quite coolly, through a set of steps which had been choreographed for me and which simply presented themselves. But even this way of recounting things lends a greater nimbus of vision to the scene than was the case. It was all very unremarkable, and I presently rejoined my wife and son, and we drove on south.

That was in August. Nothing particular followed upon this prayer until one Sunday during the fall when my wife, Lovelace, turned to me at some point in the liturgy at our (Anglican) parish church and said, "You're not here any more, are you?"

Eheu! Had this wise and godly woman seen something which I was afraid to grasp? Her words obliged me to admit that, indeed, the ground had shifted under my feet, and that I now was on the far side of the fence, looking *back* at the Anglican liturgy. "Why am I holding myself aloof from the Church of the apostles and fathers and martyrs and saints with whom I so much want to be in visible, obedient union?" I then realized that my holding back was, somehow, callow or impertinent. I do not think that those two harsh words occurred to me as applying to all the Anglicans and others of the faithful who were not in direct, visible union with the ancient Roman Church. But I felt as though *my* stance fell under this interdict, since the way in which I had come to understand this matter of the Church did present things to me in such a light—such a kindly Light, I would have said.

Kindly, yes. But terrible. Grace does not make things easy. The question "What is the Church?" which I had toyed with for so long in my study (or at least so it seemed, once it looked as though I might have to *do* something)—this question became dreadful when it emerged from the chrysalis of speculation and loomed over my actual life, commanding a decision.

My memory of the weeks following that Sunday, when Lovelace had turned to me with those alarming words, is of us sitting at the table in our kitchen (was it after breakfast, or at tea?) trying to sort things out. "What brought things to this sudden pass? What do I think I am doing? *Must* it come to a stark choice? What will we do? What about the children, who are teenagers?"

We groped along, not without tears. For one thing, Lovelace could not, in good conscience and good faith, make any such move just then: there were doctrinal and practical barriers. And for another, it would mean my leaving a whole world—the world in which my entire family and lineage had lived with great fidelity for generations. Could I really, actually, sunder myself from that world—that world of undoubted piety, nay, of seemingly matchless godliness, and of great hymns, and saintly men and women, and familiar argot, and of shared work in God's vineyard (Fundamentalism comprises a gigantic worldwide web of task forces—missions and Bible colleges and conference centers and journals and churches, right up to and including Billy Graham's whole enterprise): how could I shake the dust from my feet and leave? And look at what I proposed to choose in its place.

There was, on the one hand, the Catholicism of the books: not only the apostles and fathers and martyrs and saints and doctors of the Church, and Gregorian chant and Renaissance polyphony and the Latin Mass; but also the writers whose work had wooed and won me: Cardinal Newman, Monsignor Ronald Knox, Louis Bouyer, Flannery O'Connor, Evelyn Waugh, Romano Guardini—these all shimmered there, like a great cloud of witnesses around me. It was not that *they* had converted me, but rather that they had done their work well—of witnessing to the splendor of the ancient Faith, and of pointing *to* the truth in all of its radiance.

But on the other hand, there was the face that contemporary, local Catholicism presents. For a Protestant Fundamentalist, it is a face masking many conundrums. The faith of "your average Catholic," especially of the man or woman who has been born into the Church, and whose Catholicism is virtually indistinguishable from ethnic and folk loyalty—this is not a faith that exhibits a very reassuring face to the Protestant believer, accustomed as he is to an enormously chatty, forthcoming, Bible-quoting rendering of faith. To this man, Catholics often appear mute and even evasive about the Faith itself. You can't get them to say much about Jesus Christ, for a start, which is seriously puzzling to a Fundamentalist. "Isn't Jesus the Savior? the only Savior? *your* Savior? Shouldn't we know him, and love him, and praise him, and share him?"

The Catholic's response to this barrage is often suspicion. "Who is this zealot? What sort of an agenda have we got here? I'm a *Catholic*—isn't that enough? Don't harry me with this catechism. Ask the priest if you are so bent on getting answers."

We are all familiar with this collapse of communication, all of us on both sides of the fence. The Fundamentalist appears to the Catholic to be hailing from the lunatic fringe; and the Catholic appears to the Fundamentalist to be innocent of anything resembling "a personal relationship with Jesus Christ" (which phraseology is a sort of litmus test of faith, from the Fundamentalist point of view). Huge numbers of Catholics are, of course, just barely nominal Catholics: if there is any residue of faith anywhere in them, it is barnacled over with perfunctoriness and preoccupation with other things and generally hangdog attitudes. From this multitude, it is worth noting, come the throngs of converts *from* Catholicism *to* Protestant Fundamentalism, Pentecostalism, and evangelicalism. "I was a Catholic until I was fifteen: then I met Jesus"; or "I was a Catholic until I was seventeen, and then I became a Christian"; or "I was a Catholic until I was twenty, and then I was saved." We all know this phenomenon; and it is no doubt due to the energetic vibrancy of these forms of Protestant witness that millions of erstwhile Catholics in Brazil, the Philippines, and other countries are converting to Protestantism, leaving the Church in the backwash.

The thing that I was proposing to choose (or, more accurately, that was drawing me) was this great riddle: the Church Catholic, in all of its antiquity, authority, unity, liturgy, and sacraments, but also that Church dressed, as often as not, in the tawdry garments of contemporaneity, ethnicity, and even ignorance.

I had no illusions. It was widely supposed among people who knew me that a nostalgia for medievalism was at work. "Ah. Tom wants the thirteenth century. He wants the Rome of the great doctors in Paris, when theology was queen of sciences"; or "He wants the ostrich-plume fans and pomps and marbles of the Renaissance papacy, with the polyphony of Allegri and Palestrina."

No. Or at least no, if by that we mean that I was swept away by considerations other than the only one which will stand up when the foundations are shaken, namely, whether something is true or not. I love the Middle Ages; and I wish that Christian vision presided over civilization now as it did then; and who is immune to the soul-piercing beauty of Palestrina; and who is not awed by the sheer *might* of the basilica in Rome? But these are not reasons for pulling up your tent pegs, so to speak, and packing off for foreign parts.

From my own native region, of course, I had no way of knowing anything much about the ardor of true Catholic faith and piety as it exists in the humdrum of ordinary life for millions of faithful Catholics. I had confidence in St. Augustine, and St. Benedict, and St. Francis de Sales; and I liked the portraits of commonplace piety in Chaucer's "povre parson of the toun," and in Flannery O'Connor's Father Flynn, and in Evelyn Waugh's Gervase Crouchback. Furthermore, if I had thought about it, I would have realized that three of the men whose conversation and friendship I cherished the most were Catholics. All three of them were young professors at Boston College, and over the previous ten years I had come to admire enormously the particular *shape* which faith took in them. There seemed to be a luminousness and a serenity about it (two were philosophers, and one a psychologist): they were not forever wrestling with the (Protestant) problem of "the integration of faith and learning." There was a seamlessness in the warp and woof that bound their intellectual disciplines to their interior imagination and vision. There was nothing febrile or labored about the way they held the Faith. Moreover, they seemed to have a grasp of all sorts of things that no one in my own background knew anything about: the evangelical counsels; the corporal works of mercy; the two kinds of grace; the cardinal virtues; the six traditional precepts of the Church; and so forth. The Faith had for them a solidity and an *order* that eluded most of the efforts I had made.

And beyond this, again, if I had thought about it, I would have realized that the two figures in the modern world who embodied the Christian Faith in the eyes of us all were Mother

Teresa of Calcutta and Pope John Paul II. If Mother Teresa was not ministering Jesus to the poor and dying (*and* to Harvard, in her graduation address there), then nobody was. And how earnestly we all looked to the Bishop of Rome in these troubling days, with the confidence that he would speak to us the apostolic Faith with utter clarity and fidelity.

And little did I know of the joyous, articulate, ebullient even, Catholic piety which I would encounter at Franciscan University of Steubenville, Ohio, within a year or two of my being received into the Church. Not one of your watering-spots, if we are speaking of the tourist industry: but a locale where the word "Catholic" takes on all the vitality and ardor and articulateness for which I longed, and where Marian piety, far from detracting from the Christocentric nature of the Faith, is the very handmaiden of true Christocentrism.

As Lovelace and I struggled and talked and prayed all through that autumn of 1984, the tug of war inside of me was between "Am I mad?" and "Show me, dear Christ, Thy spouse so bright and clear." Could I introduce this fissure into our very household? How could I possibly head for a Table other than the one at which my dear lady made her communion from week to week, and at which I had brought up my children and, indeed, at which I myself had worshipped for twenty-five years? And could I jeopardize my own livelihood, I, a middle-aged man obliged to keep bread on his family's table?

There was something inexorable about the whole business. It was as though I stood on a threshold, and that the door now stood open before me. I am not a man given to heroic gestures. Quite the opposite. Just let me get on with it (life, I suppose) without causing trauma and tempest. Just let me make it to my grave—or, so go my thoughts often; but who knows himself well enough to know whether this is his authentic voice, or only one of many clamoring characters in his own self, with other voices egging him on to "Go! Make a splash! Ginger life up with some drama!" Self-knowledge eludes us— even when we spend years, and all of our substance, in pursuing it at the hands of the experts. The Christian gospel indicates that self-absorption is disastrous and will, eventually, land us in the sad and squalid solitude of hell. So I would not be prepared to claim that my motives were all entirely clear, or that I moved with the stainless integrity which we find in the saints. But, even acknowledging the jumble that obtains in one's inner being, I would have to testify, in retrospect, that there was something inexorable about the matter. The only other occasion in my life which has unfolded with such clarity, and which has been, in the event, ratified and validated gloriously and incalculably, was my decision to ask Lovelace to marry me. There have been no second thoughts about that one in the thirty years that have elapsed (and, jumping ahead of my narrative here, the same has proved true in the nine years since I was received into the Church).

The single event which changed everything at a stroke that autumn was Lovelace's saying to me one day, quite unanticipatedly, "I have to tell you that the Lord has enabled me not simply to endure what you have resolved to do, nor even merely to 'affirm' it neutrally: He has given me Wings of Joy about it. I want this to be the happiest day in your life." (I capitalize those two words, since that is how they exist in my imagination.)

Not only am I not one given to heroic gestures: I do not live my life among signs, wonders, and miracles. But this word from my lady was as stark a "sign" as I have ever experienced. It was, I would wish to testify, the "word of the Lord" to me at that most frightening part of the pilgrimage. I could now move.

I rang up a friend with, "Ted—is there any such thing as a priest who could talk to me about my being received into the Church?" "Oh—I have the very man for you!"

And so I was put in touch with the legendary "Father Sal" Ferigle, a Spanish priest who had lived in America since the 1940s, and who, to all who know him, is a fountainhead of wisdom, grace, and sanctity. He agreed to meet with this inquirer—yet another straggler among the hundreds whom he has helped to shepherd into the Fold.

On December 31, 1984, I made my last communion as an Anglican at our parish church in Hamilton, Massachusetts. On January 1, 1985, I went into St. Margaret's Church in Beverly Farms, where we now lived, for Mass.

I could not, of course, make my communion: but from January 1 until the Easter Vigil of that year, I was present at Mass in this church from week to week.

7

Becoming Catholic

On one evening each week I would drive in to Boston to meet with Father Sal. He recognized that the prescription for me was not the usual course of instruction offered by the Church to catechumens and candidates, since I had been instructed in the Bible since infancy, and had been reading Church history and Catholic theology and spirituality for the last twenty-five years. But he patiently agreed to hear my questions.

I had, I suppose, the inevitable questions. While the Mass and even the papacy presented no difficulties for me, I could not yet find my way through the Marian doctrines, most notably the Immaculate Conception and the Assumption. The nub of my difficulties here was my residual adherence to the Protestant (and non-biblical) notion of *sola Scriptura*. The Bible alone. And surely, from this point of view, the Marian doctrines are outrageous. "Where is the verse in the New Testament that teaches *that*?"

goes the question ordinarily. And put that way, of course, the question begs the question.

The Catholic Church teaches, as did the early bishops and fathers, that revelation has come to us supremely and finally in the Incarnation of the Word, and that revelation is then given, taught, and guarded by the Church, which both wrote and ratified the Bible. The Church has no warrant to cobble up quirky and adventitious doctrines *ex nihilo;* but the Church, reflecting on revelation and on the whole mystery of the gospel, unfolds doctrine organically from century to century under the authority and constraint of the Holy Spirit. The believers, for example, had only imperfect notions about the mystery of our Lord's two natures in the early years; but at the early councils, in Ephesus, Chalcedon, and Nicaea, this doctrine was articulated, made explicit, and settled forever for Catholic orthodoxy. It does not constitute an addition to Scripture; but neither is it made explicit in any single passage of Scripture. The Church reflected on the revelation of God in Christ, and hammered out the doctrine of our Lord's divine and human natures in one person. Very difficult words were brought into play, most notably the famous *homoousion*, as opposed to the (heretical) *homoiousion*. "Where is the simplicity of the primitive Gospel!" a peasant zealot might cry out. "You are confusing us with mere theology!" The Church's only answer to this earnest appeal is that the work of theology, thankless as it may sound and pettifogging as it may appear, is nevertheless one part of the whole pastoral office of the Church. What is it that we worship when we worship Jesus Christ in the liturgy? He is God and Man.

By the same token, no one knows exactly what appreciation the first disciples had of Mary, the Mother of Jesus. Certainly they knew her well; and she was present at all the significant events—the Annunciation, Nativity, Crucifixion, the Resurrection, Pentecost. Whether this company of fledgling believers had much grasp of her unique participation in the drama of redemption is unrecorded. But as the early Church reflected on her part in the whole mystery, it was able to appreciate, and then to spell out, more and more of what her part was. By AD 431, at the Council of Ephesus, the Church had officially recognized her as *Theotokos*, the God-bearer (thus safeguarding the doctrine of Christ, who was God-in-the-flesh, and not just a most excellent teacher or unique prophet).

This process of the living Church attending closely to the words of revelation in Scripture and reflecting century by century on the mystery of Faith is what has given us Tradition. Non-Catholics often fear that Tradition entails a shelving of the Bible, and a turning to a second, separate source (the imaginations of mere men) for doctrine. Not so. Scripture and Tradition cannot be sundered any more than hydrogen and oxygen can be sundered if we want water, or any more than Bread and Wine can be sundered in the Eucharist. To drive a wedge between the two and raise the slogan *Sola Scriptura!* like a banner is to do violence to Scripture by making it what it itself never claimed to be. "He will guide you into all truth"—the Church hears these words of the Lord about the Holy Spirit, and takes them at their full solemnity; "the pillar and ground of the truth"—so St. Paul speaks of the Church: that is, the Holy Spirit working in and through the Church. The huge tree, big enough for all the birds of heaven to roost in, grown from the smallest of seeds, is the picture. Spiritually, geographically, pastorally, doctrinally, the Church has grown immeasurably. To want to return to the picture of the infant Church in the book of Acts, which is often urged by ardent sectarians as over against the titanic size, say, of the holy Catholic Church, is to want to return to the acorn when what we have here is a gigantic oak. That seed was a healthy, living seed, and it has been tended by a husbandman who is understood by the Church to be *Dominum et Vivificantem*—the Lord and Giver of Life, namely, the Holy Spirit. The Church was not stillborn, pastorally, spiritually, or doctrinally.

It is into some such picture as this that the rich Marian doctrines are to be placed. The Gospels and Epistles tell us little of her. Biographical information is scant indeed. But the Church's understanding of her unique role as the vessel by means of which salvation was given to our world has unfolded gradually and organically through the centuries. The Church knows and heeds St. Paul's words to Timothy that "there is one God, and one mediator between God and man, the man Christ Jesus." Mary as intercessor, and even Mediatrix, does not mean that Catholicism has insinuated this woman into Christ's place and obliged him to move over ever so slightly. Rather the Church sees in her the great mystery in which we find that God *draws us in* to the operations of grace, allowing us mortals to "fill up that which is behind of the suffering of Christ," and to be "crucified with" him, and ourselves to be the flesh-and-blood vessels (sub-mediators, as it were) by which grace is conveyed to our race. Any preacher or evangelist is in this rudimentary sense a "mediator" in that *he* is the voice they hear uttering the Word of God; and any intercessor among us, far from interposing *his* prayers in between Christ's all-sufficient intercessory priesthood and me, say, who has asked for my brother's prayers—any intercessor is, to this extent, a "mediator"—not a second mediator, but rather one who has been drawn into the unique priesthood of our One High Priest and Mediator.

The Virgin Mary is seen as being at the forefront of this mystery. Her office as Mediatrix and intercessor is "nothing but" her participation in the mediatorship and intercession of Jesus Christ, the One Priest. She is the great sign, then, of God's superabundant grace, whereby he draws his people into the very thing he is doing for their salvation. Obviously her role is unique. No other creature in the universe, up to and including the seraphim, has been crowned with the dignity which crowns this woman, for no one else has been drawn so closely into the divine plan of salvation. Patriarchs, prophets, apostles, kings, angels—these all bore witness *to* the Word; *Mary bore the Word.* No wonder the angel hails her as highly exalted.

But my task here is not to expound doctrine. Questions about all of this were in the forefront of my mind as I went to Father Sal from week to week. And I cannot pretend that I managed to settle everything in a manner which laid my questions altogether to rest. On certain points I had to step down, as it were, from my unwitting, self-appointed role as arbiter and judge of all doctrine, and remind myself that I had, indeed, become convinced that the Catholic Church is the Church, and that there was a sense in which a man may have to "hand over" to that Church the final responsibility for doctrine. Within the circumference of what might be called good faith, a man could say, "I have become convinced that the Catholic Church is the Church. This (Doctrine A, B, or C) is what she teaches. I will make my obedience to this Church and continue in this pilgrimage of faith in which the light shines brighter and brighter unto the perfect day." Something like that. It was analogous, in my mind, to the attitude I had always had toward hell as a Fundamentalist. "Do you sincerely believe that the wicked dead will leap and writhe in agony forever?" someone might have taxed me with; and my only response would have been, "I believe the Bible is the Word of God. *I* didn't make up the doctrine of hell, and I don't have to answer for it. Certainly I have no warrant to *expunge* it from revelation.

So—whatever it means, yes, I would submit to the authority of the Bible." This attitude avoids the error of setting oneself up as judge of matters that are infinitely beyond one's powers; but it does not presume to nail down too ferociously just what the doctrine might mean.

It was this way with the Marian doctrines for me at this point. *Did* I believe that she had been conceived without sin? My lifelong (Protestant) imagination balked. Was my loyalty to the Bible being called into question? But here was the apostolic Church (which received and ratified the Bible) teaching this about the Virgin's role in the drama of salvation. Right: I will take my place in the great train of the faithful, from Pentecost on down, and see myself as a pupil, not a teacher.

If I seem to have diverted from my narrative into immense expanses of doctrine, I would urge that the space I have given to this sort of thing at this point in my narrative is, in fact, a fairly accurate rendering of what my experience was like in those early months of 1985 as I met from week to week with Father Sal. I was almost wholly preoccupied with this daunting task of *becoming Catholic.*

8

Shuffling across the Threshold with Wings of Joy

Eventually Easter approached, and with it the Great Vigil of Easter—that holy time at the end of Holy Saturday, on the eve of the Resurrection, when the Church, from the beginning, has gathered most solemnly to bear witness to our passage in Christ, out from the Egypt of our bondage to sin, across the Red Sea of deliverance, and into the Promised Land of salvation. It is at this time that the Church has, again from the beginning, received catechumens by baptism into full participation in the mystery of the Church, and hence, into full communion with the Church at the Eucharist.

I had already been baptized many years before as a Christian believer, so the Church did not ask me to be re-baptized. But I was to take my place in the lineup before the bishop to have apostolic hands laid on me, and to hear the words spoken by the Church, receiving me as a Catholic.

On the morning of Holy Saturday I was working in my study at home when the phone rang. A man's voice said, "Hello, Tom?" "Yes," I said. "This is Archbishop [now Cardinal] Law. Could you by any chance come and have lunch with me today?"

I allowed as how I could make room in my schedule for the archbishop, and duly drove to his residence in Brighton. He received me most warmly. There was a cardinal from the Roman Curia visiting him that day, so the three of us had lunch in the dining room at the residence, waited on by what one of my Irish friends calls "the wee nuns." I am embarrassed as I think back on the conversation at the table, however. I recall descanting volubly on this and that, innocent of the reticence that ought to govern one in the presence of two princes of the Church. They were long-suffering, and never by the smallest lift of an archiepiscopal eyebrow betrayed anything but the keenest interest in this cavalier and prolix convert.

How had my ordinary got wind of my imminent entry into the Church? To this day I do not know. But his gesture toward me has stayed in my mind as an extraordinarily generous instance of true pastoral care. Here was this anxious middle-aged man about to take this step:

perhaps he would be encouraged by a word from his ordinary.

That evening my wife and son and daughter drove with me to St. Aidan's Church in Brookline (Boston), where I was to be received. It is a church that might be mistaken for an Episcopal church (was this the Divine Mercy tempering the wind to the shorn lamb?), all stone and dark timbers and gothic lines. Father Sal and Father Coppenrath, the pastor, met me, and I joined the group of catechumens in the parish hall. There was a photographer there from evangelicalism's principal journal, and she took pictures of me kneeling in the empty nave, which presently appeared in that journal along with full coverage of the event, the burden of which was to the effect that Tom Howard has become a Roman Catholic, but nobody needs to worry too much since the following are the points at which Catholicism is heretical: one, two, three, four, and so forth.

A number of my friends and former students arrived for the Vigil. As the liturgy began with the striking of the new fire and the procession with the Paschal Candle, and then the Exsultet and all of the glorious readings from the Old Testament, I found a great jumble in my own emotions: this was the culmination of a long pilgrimage; and it was also a daunting beginning; and it was also a farewell to all that was familiar. Fright was, I think, the dominant note, as I suppose it will be if I am conscious at the moment of my death which will also be a long-looked-for culmination, a beginning, and a farewell. On the other hand, to find oneself moving through the steps through which catechumens have moved since apostolic and patristic times at this liturgy, and to be borne along by readings, canticles, ritual, and ceremony of immemorial antiquity and dignity, is to be—well, *borne along*. One is clearly not flying off on one's own. One is not joining some late-arriving cult. Despite one's inner anxiety, one is making a move as sure as birth, marriage, and death—and one which is as profoundly an event in human existence as are those three transactions.

One small aspect of the proceedings jogged my elbow with a salutary jog as I took my place in the line-up of catechumens in front of the bishop (a retired bishop who, I found later, is a veritable pillar of orthodoxy): nearly all of the others in the line were either children, or foreign-born, non-Saxon folks. "Hey nonny," I thought. "There's no preferential option for fifty-year-old Nordic academic males in Christ's one, holy, catholic, and apostolic Church. Hum. Here is matter to be mulled over. This is what the Kingdom of Heaven is like."

The moment when the bishop's hands were laid on my head was, I found, not unlike other crucial moments—the moment of marriage, say, or even of one's receiving the Eucharistic wafer: one submits to something rather brief, in the external, physical world, and one's inner grasp of the sheer size of it scarcely answers to its solemnity; and yet one's intellect assents. Neither the significance nor the validity of the event depends in the smallest degree on the adequacy of one's own emotional response. *Ex opere operato.*

A local Catholic family from the prelature Opus Dei had invited me and all of the friends who had come to the Vigil to come to their apartment afterwards for champagne and sandwiches. I felt embraced, as it were, and received. The Church had officially (and warmly) received me: now the laity welcomed me.

A certain amount of flurry occurred in the public realm. I had a minor visibility in Fundamentalist circles, since I had written books and articles which had had limited circulation. People also knew of me because my family had been active in Fundamentalism for a hundred years. For a scion of this house to "pope," as they used to say in England, was looked upon as perhaps newsworthy.

The local papers sent reporters to interview me. As a result of the articles which appeared locally, I found myself answering eager letters and phone calls from Catholics in the neighborhood, welcoming me warmly and assuring me of their prayers. A few of the nationally-circulated Catholic journals picked up the scent, and letters arrived from all over North America, some of them saying literally, "Welcome! Welcome! Welcome!" I was enrolled in so many rosters to be prayed for at Mass that I wondered what the Lord *did* with a volume of prayers like this.

I had to relinquish my position as professor of English at a nearby evangelical college. The college had a vigorous and vibrant Protestant tradition, and had never had a Catholic on the faculty. Its clientele was, largely, deeply mistrustful of Catholicism; and for the college to have kept on a man who had switched horses of such importance in midstream would have resulted in a confusion which I myself would not wish to have brought upon the college.

There was a paradox, of course, since all of us, even the few members of the faculty who most strenuously urged that it would not do for me to continue—all of us knew that we were speaking as deeply-committed Christian brothers. The simplistic bystander, with breezy good will, might easily have urged that differences be swept under the rug and that we all step ahead with bold ecumenical vision. But things rarely happen with such swift decisiveness, and we mortals must bumble along with things as they have been handed to us. Neither the college nor I had created the five hundred years of trouble between Catholicism and Protestantism, and we could not make it all evaporate.

Many of the faculty and the administration were clearly deeply distressed by the inevitable (my leaving); but we all knew that, of the options, this was the realistic and charitable one. For my part, I would have to bear witness that there was not a shade of bad faith, duplicity, or pusillanimity. What occurred, occurred with good faith on all sides, I think.

So I resigned my professorship of fifteen years.

To find oneself out in the street at age fifty is alarming. An aging candidate like me, top-heavy with rank and tenure, would be virtually unhire-able in the view of any academic dean anywhere, or so I thought. So I conjured, in my fevered and hasty imagination, pictures of me selling apples on the street corner, or mopping floors at the local hospital (this latter was the picture I fixed upon as most appropriate).

To add to the melancholy cast of things, I had to undergo minor surgery that summer after my resignation. This left me in bed, weakened, with time on my hands, staring at the ceiling. Faith has a way of draining away in periods like this; and I thought I knew how Hagar and Elijah and Jonah and Jeremiah and John the Baptist felt at the points when they concluded that God had forgotten them. The image of the Holy Family wending their forlorn way down into Egypt, after all the *Gloria in excelsis Deo* that had gilded things for them briefly, presented itself to me. "Ha, ha!" jeers the Tempter in one's ear. "Look at where your little drama has landed you!"

As I lay there in my bedroom dilating on this line of thought, in through the door walked a man in a Roman collar. "Hi. I'm Jerry Dorgan. I teach at St. John's Seminary. Would you like to teach for us?"

"Yes."

"Praise the Lord!"

That is, literally and without embellishment, what was said.

To my surprise, the archdiocesan seminary had got word of things and had issued this invitation. It was, specifically, that I teach a course in Dante on a part-time basis in the undergraduate house of the seminary (Catholic seminary, not infrequently, is an eight-year business, the first four years being the men's undergraduate work—college, in other words—with the second four years being their theology work proper). This invitation meant that I could simply go on doing what I had always done and loved, namely, teaching undergraduate literature courses.

I was embarrassed, of course, at my own swiftness in concluding that God had forgotten me. Grace knows, we are told, how much we can bear, and may have concluded in my case that mopping floors was a discipline for which I was not yet ready. In any event, I was not asked to undergo the long, bleak, enervating ordeal of being without work. What began as a part-time position fairly quickly became a full-time position, and as I write this manuscript, I am still on the faculty at the seminary.

One element in the story which remains unknown to me is a possible hand which Cardinal Law had in helping me. Did he say to the seminary, "Can you find this man a slot?" I don't know, but I suspect that he may have. Certainly he had been astonishingly pastoral to me personally.

9

A Newcomer's Discoveries

So the narrative which has led from my child-hood up to the point of my being received into the ancient Church comes to a close, as it were. I say "as it were" since, of course, that Easter Vigil was the beginning. What have I found now that I have been a Catholic for nine years? What have I learned?

For one thing, I have begun to learn about plenitude. That is, I have been the beneficiary of the Church's "fullness," expressed in multitudinous apostolates and charisms.

For example, at the time of my being received one of the phone calls which came in was from one Sister Catherine D'Arcy, a Notre Dame sister. She herself was now retired from her school teaching and was confined to a wheel-chair. But she flooded me and my family with largesse, both material and spiritual. We would drive over to the convent in Ipswich, Massachusetts, where she lived. There she would be, bustling with welcome, good cheer, solicitude, and generosity. Every time we went she would have gifts for all of us—on one occasion there were two shopping bags full of presents. She had no interest in her own numerous physical ailments, but only inquiries and prayers for every detail of our family life.

And again, a nearby convent of discalced Carmelite nuns virtually adopted us all. We would go and visit with them in the "speak room," with the grille between them and us. Joy, joy, joy radiated from them into our very marrow. They took us into their hearts, and have prayed for us from that day until now. None of us, I think, has ever encountered sheer Charity in any more dazzling manifestation than we have from these nuns.

And what else have I learned?

The answer to that would run to many pages—to book length, really; and since it would entail many things which I, the newcomer, have scarcely begun to descry, there would be something headlong about my descanting this early in the game on the ancient Church and all that it holds for us in its liturgy, its teaching, its disciplines, its devotions, and its spiritual writings.

Nevertheless, it may not be altogether inappropriate for a newcomer to list a very few of the rudimentary impressions which have hailed his consciousness in these first years. To number them rather than to attempt a systematic sequence will perhaps remind readers that the items constitute ad hoc jottings, so to speak.

1. The holy Catholic Church looks more like the five thousand whom the Lord fed on the hillside than it does the small group of insiders in the Upper Room. That is, everyone is here: the earnest and the preoccupied; the poor and the rich; the fashionable and the unfashionable (more of the latter than the former); the ignorant and the luminously wise; the proletariat and the bourgeoisie (to reach for anachronistic categories); the pathetic and the impressive. It is just "us" whom this very ancient Church comprises. None of us has any credentials at all other than the fact that we are baptized into this Church.

2. The Catholic Faith is, mysteriously, "higher" and "deeper" than the rendering of the Christian Faith encountered in quarters of Christendom of more recent lineage. That is, one finds the shimmering massif of Augustine, Anselm, Bonaventure, and Thomas (*and*, one might add, of Newman and von Balthasar and Dietrich von Hildebrand and Romano Guardini), but, at the other apparent extreme ("apparent" because the two extremes participate profoundly

in the same mystery), the local and folk and ethnic piety which has clearly risen quite
spontaneously from the genius of various
peoples. I am thinking of tiny wayside shrines
in Austria, and Mardi Gras, and the St. Anthony's
gala festival which I used to see when I lived in
New York City, and the strange, heart-piercing
flamenco singing which one hears in Madrid as
great floats carrying the Virgin struggle through
the streets on the backs of scores of barefoot
penitents. Much of this looks grotesque, even
pagan, to non-Catholics, and no doubt supersti-
tion or mere festivity is not infrequently at work.
But it would be perilous to dismiss these phe-
nomena too summarily. The sense in which grace
may, oddly, be truly at work in the midst of all
the clutter should hinder the bystander from
harsh judgments. *Pieta*s and *caritas* take strange
and scandalous forms often, and because, according to Catholic understanding, grace builds
on nature, it is inevitable that the experience of
grace will display itself in multitudinous and
extravagant ways. Remember the uncouth
woman who interrupted a dinner party and wept
all over the Lord's feet and wasted all the nard?
This sort of thing eludes the categories of Christians who espouse a rigorously verbalist,
propositionalist, non-sacramental rendering of
the Faith.

3. Faith is virtually unrecognizable, often, across the barriers that crisscross Christendom. That is, your muttering Balkan crone in a babushka kissing the icon of the Mother of God of Kazan is not going to be able to convince a young North American evangelical, accustomed as he is to energetic Bible studies and "fellowship" and expertise in extempore prayer, that she is, in fact, a *Christian*. Her mute and perplexed response to his catechizing ("Are you born again?" "Do you know Jesus personally?") will convince him that his worst suspicions have been correct, and that all of these peasants who are so numerous in Orthodoxy and Catholicism must be numbered among the superstitious rather than among the faithful. And, of course, we do not have to go as far as the Balkans: the congregation at Mass in any parish church on any day of the year will comprise everyone from advanced saints to people whose conversation is laced with profanity and vulgarity, and whose whole approach to life, from one perspective, excludes even the smallest trace of anything that can be recognized as faith. Where are these latter people—inside or outside of the pale of faith? Only God knows. The Church's task is to woo them, and to keep on in its pastoral efforts to fan any minuscule and lambent flicker of faith,

and to keep offering them the gospel in word and sacrament. If they consciously and explicitly reject it all, then the Church can only pray for them: "Lord Jesus Christ, forgive us our sins, save us from the fires of hell, and lead all souls to heaven, especially those most in need of thy mercy." If judgment must fall on any of them (or on me), the Church must accompany them all the way to the block, as it were, with the appeals of grace.

Some such attitude on the part of the Catholic Church, surely, must explain why she goes ahead and furnishes Christian burial to, say, those Mafiosi who have been busy murdering their rivals on Saturday nights: only God knows what seedling of faith might still be alive in the burly corruption. The Church shares God's seeking of the lost, not his office as Judge.

4. "Trouble," especially doctrinal conflict and the various efforts to include moral (read "sexual") innovations within the pale of the Church, is qualitatively different in the Catholic Church from what it is in the denominations in Christendom which have abandoned their link with the apostolic teaching authority of the Petrine See in Rome. In church X, shall we say, we may find a bishop urging homosexuality as a profoundly Christian "style of life," or osten-

tatiously doubting the Lord's virgin birth, or busily eroding the confidence of his flock in the text of Scripture. Nothing can be done except ad hoc protest. Good men in the denomination may get up a White Paper, or write articles, or introduce a resolution in the next General Convention. But we all know what this sort of thing ends in. Alas. In the Catholic Church there occurs this same heresy and false teaching, often loudly taught in high theological quarters. But everyone—both in the world and the Church—knows that there is a desk on which the buck stops, so to speak, and that when Rome has spoken on the issue, it is concluded. Oh, to be sure, Father C. or Father F. over here can keep on burbling—Rome cannot stop that. But Rome can say and does say to the Church and the world, "This which you hear Fathers C. and F. teaching is not Catholic teaching. It is not in accord with the Faith once for all delivered to us by the apostles." A pressure group organized by trendy nuns in favor of abortion exists explicitly in rebellion against what Rome teaches. No one need be in the slightest doubt on the point; whereas another denomination, if it can ever get up the votes, can only pass a resolution. The Archbishop of Canterbury himself has not in our lifetime said, "No. That is heresy." Rome has. (See *Veritatis Splendor*, the encyclical letter from

John Paul II "To all the bishops of the Catholic Church regarding certain fundamental questions of the Church's moral teaching." August 6, 1993.)

5. Catholics typically do not have a notion of "my relationship with the Lord," as do so many of their fellow-believers in evangelical Protestantism, which exists independently of their attendance at Mass, their praying the rosary, going to confession, and so forth. For Catholics these activities constitute the daily shape which such a relationship takes. They meet the Lord in the Eucharist; they hear the Bible—great dollops of it—at the liturgy (which is where the early Church visualized the Bible's characteristic usage to lie); they pray, privately and extemporaneously, as well as communally in the liturgy, and by using the rosary. In this connection it would be an excellent thing for non-Catholics to refrain altogether from assessing whether the rosary is a legitimate, and even rich, mode of prayer. The rosary constitutes a discipline which is entirely unimaginable to one who is a stranger to it. The most common objection from outsiders is that the rosary is a matter of "vain repetition as the heathen do." The remark, biblical though it may be, is nothing to the purpose here. Where the rosary is

sincerely and regularly prayed, you find ardent piety and pure devotion to the Lord. The rosary cannot coexist with cynicism, worldliness, unbelief, pride, and concupiscence. I have discovered this to be true, and the discovery has exposed any former strictures which I might ever have advanced against the rosary to be what they were—callow, ignorant, ill-conceived.

6.   To be Catholic is to be delivered, once for all, from the obligation to hoist any special banner, or to claim allegiance to any particular and recent rendering of the Faith. To be sure, one looks in a special way to an earthly, historical city, namely Rome. But there is a difference of more than a greater number of years belonging to Rome than to Geneva, Zurich, Amsterdam, Herrnhut, Canterbury, or Anderson, Indiana. There was no Peter, Paul, Linus, Cletus, or Clement in any of these latter cities. The Church universal has never said, *"Geneva locuta est"* (Geneva has spoken) when it came to doctrinal definitions. But to pit one city against another in this way is to arouse partisanship and factional cries. That is ill-gotten among Christians. My point is only that the only history which we Christians do have in this world (and we get only one "go" at history), very early on, settled upon this city as literally the locale and seat of pasto-

ral authority for the universal Church. Like Augustine with the Donatists in his day, Catholics may have profound sympathy with any number of the "protests" that have been mounted against corruption, falsehood, worldliness, or sin in the Catholic Church. As Augustine would teach us to say, "Alas: your criticism is too true. There may be wounds and bruises and putrefying sores, from the crown of the head to the soles of the feet; but we cannot dismember and hack to pieces the Body of Christ." This has been done in the last five hundred years. We have no warrant to set ourselves over against this ancient Church. There may be among us wolves in sheep's clothing, even; yet the answer to that is not to leave the Fold, but to cleanse and protect and restore it. God bless the earnestness and fidelity and zeal with which many have striven for righteousness and truth and purity in the Church. But insofar as their striving has separated them from that old Church, then the measures have been too draconian. To pray with the Lord in his prayer recorded in John 17 *may* be to do more than voice a petition. It may, in this latter day, mean a difficult obedience.